# 50 Classic Cookie Recipes for Home

By: Kelly Johnson

# Table of Contents

- Chocolate Chip Cookies
- Oatmeal Raisin Cookies
- Peanut Butter Cookies
- Snickerdoodles
- Sugar Cookies
- Double Chocolate Cookies
- Gingerbread Cookies
- Shortbread Cookies
- Almond Biscotti
- Thumbprint Jam Cookies
- White Chocolate Macadamia Nut Cookies
- Molasses Cookies
- Lemon Butter Cookies
- Coconut Macaroons
- Linzer Cookies
- Chocolate Crinkle Cookies
- Meringue Cookies
- Italian Wedding Cookies
- Peanut Butter Blossoms
- Pecan Sandies
- Black and White Cookies
- Rugelach
- Spritz Cookies
- Anzac Biscuits
- Butter Pecan Cookies
- No-Bake Chocolate Oatmeal Cookies
- Raspberry Almond Thumbprints
- Pumpkin Spice Cookies
- Cinnamon Sugar Palmiers
- Florentine Lace Cookies
- Honey Lavender Shortbread
- Viennese Whirls
- Chocolate-Dipped Coconut Cookies
- Tahini Sesame Cookies
- Apple Cider Cookies

- Bourbon Pecan Cookies
- Cornmeal Lime Cookies
- Chocolate-Dipped Orange Biscotti
- Hazelnut Crescent Cookies
- Banana Oatmeal Cookies
- Maple Walnut Cookies
- Matcha Green Tea Cookies
- Brown Butter Chocolate Chip Cookies
- White Chocolate Cranberry Cookies
- Classic Whoopie Pies
- Peanut Butter Oatmeal Cookies
- Espresso Chocolate Cookies
- Red Velvet Crinkle Cookies
- Caramel-Stuffed Chocolate Cookies
- S'mores Cookies

## Chocolate Chip Cookies

*Ingredients:*

- 1 cup (226g) unsalted butter, softened
- 1 cup (200g) brown sugar
- ½ cup (100g) granulated sugar
- 2 eggs
- 1 teaspoon vanilla extract
- 2 ½ cups (315g) all-purpose flour
- 1 teaspoon baking soda
- ½ teaspoon salt
- 2 cups (340g) chocolate chips

*Instructions:*

1. **Preheat oven** to 350°F (175°C).
2. **Mix wet ingredients:** Beat butter, sugars, eggs, and vanilla.
3. **Combine dry ingredients:** Mix flour, baking soda, and salt, then add to wet ingredients.
4. **Fold in chocolate chips.**
5. **Bake** for 10-12 minutes until golden brown.

**Oatmeal Raisin Cookies**

*Ingredients:*

- 1 cup (226g) unsalted butter, softened
- 1 cup (200g) brown sugar
- ½ cup (100g) granulated sugar
- 2 eggs
- 1 teaspoon vanilla extract
- 2 cups (180g) rolled oats
- 1 ½ cups (190g) all-purpose flour
- 1 teaspoon baking soda
- 1 teaspoon cinnamon
- 1 cup (150g) raisins

*Instructions:*

1. **Preheat oven** to 350°F (175°C).
2. **Mix wet ingredients:** Beat butter, sugars, eggs, and vanilla.
3. **Combine dry ingredients:** Mix flour, baking soda, and cinnamon, then add to wet ingredients.
4. **Fold in oats and raisins.**
5. **Bake** for 10-12 minutes.

## Peanut Butter Cookies

*Ingredients:*

- 1 cup (256g) peanut butter
- ½ cup (113g) unsalted butter, softened
- ¾ cup (150g) brown sugar
- ½ cup (100g) granulated sugar
- 1 egg
- 1 teaspoon vanilla extract
- 1 ½ cups (190g) all-purpose flour
- 1 teaspoon baking soda
- ½ teaspoon salt

*Instructions:*

1. **Preheat oven** to 350°F (175°C).
2. **Mix wet ingredients:** Beat peanut butter, butter, sugars, egg, and vanilla.
3. **Combine dry ingredients:** Mix flour, baking soda, and salt, then add to wet ingredients.
4. **Form dough into balls and press with a fork.**
5. **Bake** for 10-12 minutes.

## Snickerdoodles

*Ingredients:*

- 1 cup (226g) unsalted butter, softened
- 1 ½ cups (300g) granulated sugar
- 2 eggs
- 1 teaspoon vanilla extract
- 2 ¾ cups (345g) all-purpose flour
- 1 teaspoon baking soda
- 1 teaspoon cream of tartar
- ½ teaspoon salt
- 2 tablespoons sugar + 1 teaspoon cinnamon (for rolling)

*Instructions:*

1. **Preheat oven** to 375°F (190°C).
2. **Mix wet ingredients:** Beat butter, sugar, eggs, and vanilla.
3. **Combine dry ingredients:** Mix flour, baking soda, cream of tartar, and salt, then add to wet ingredients.
4. **Roll dough balls in cinnamon sugar.**
5. **Bake** for 10-12 minutes.

**Sugar Cookies**

*Ingredients:*

- 1 cup (226g) unsalted butter, softened
- 1 cup (200g) granulated sugar
- 1 egg
- 1 teaspoon vanilla extract
- 2 ½ cups (315g) all-purpose flour
- 1 teaspoon baking powder
- ½ teaspoon salt

*Instructions:*

1. **Preheat oven** to 350°F (175°C).
2. **Mix wet ingredients:** Beat butter, sugar, egg, and vanilla.
3. **Combine dry ingredients:** Mix flour, baking powder, and salt, then add to wet ingredients.
4. **Roll out dough, cut into shapes.**
5. **Bake** for 8-10 minutes.

**Double Chocolate Cookies**

*Ingredients:*

- 1 cup (226g) unsalted butter, softened
- 1 cup (200g) brown sugar
- ½ cup (100g) granulated sugar
- 2 eggs
- 1 teaspoon vanilla extract
- 2 cups (250g) all-purpose flour
- ½ cup (60g) cocoa powder
- 1 teaspoon baking soda
- ½ teaspoon salt
- 2 cups (340g) chocolate chips

*Instructions:*

1. **Preheat oven** to 350°F (175°C).
2. **Mix wet ingredients:** Beat butter, sugars, eggs, and vanilla.
3. **Combine dry ingredients:** Mix flour, cocoa, baking soda, and salt, then add to wet ingredients.
4. **Fold in chocolate chips.**
5. **Bake** for 10-12 minutes.

## Gingerbread Cookies

*Ingredients:*

- ¾ cup (170g) unsalted butter, softened
- ¾ cup (150g) brown sugar
- ½ cup (120ml) molasses
- 1 egg
- 2 ¾ cups (345g) all-purpose flour
- 1 teaspoon baking soda
- 1 tablespoon ginger
- 1 teaspoon cinnamon
- ½ teaspoon cloves
- ½ teaspoon salt

*Instructions:*

1. **Preheat oven** to 350°F (175°C).
2. **Mix wet ingredients:** Beat butter, sugar, molasses, and egg.
3. **Combine dry ingredients:** Mix flour, baking soda, spices, and salt, then add to wet ingredients.
4. **Roll out dough, cut into shapes.**
5. **Bake** for 10-12 minutes.

## Shortbread Cookies

***Ingredients:***

- 1 cup (226g) unsalted butter, softened
- ½ cup (100g) granulated sugar
- 2 ½ cups (315g) all-purpose flour
- ½ teaspoon salt

***Instructions:***

1. **Preheat oven** to 325°F (165°C).
2. **Mix ingredients:** Beat butter and sugar, then mix in flour and salt.
3. **Form dough, roll out, and cut into shapes.**
4. **Bake** for 15-18 minutes.

## Almond Biscotti

*Ingredients:*

- 2 cups (250g) all-purpose flour
- ¾ cup (150g) sugar
- 1 teaspoon baking powder
- ½ teaspoon salt
- 2 eggs
- 1 teaspoon almond extract
- 1 cup (140g) almonds, chopped

*Instructions:*

1. **Preheat oven** to 350°F (175°C).
2. **Mix ingredients:** Beat eggs, sugar, and almond extract. Mix in flour, baking powder, and salt. Stir in almonds.
3. **Shape into logs and bake for 25 minutes.**
4. **Slice logs and bake again for 10 minutes.**

## Thumbprint Jam Cookies

*Ingredients:*

- 1 cup (226g) unsalted butter, softened
- ½ cup (100g) granulated sugar
- 2 cups (250g) all-purpose flour
- ½ teaspoon salt
- ½ cup (120g) jam

*Instructions:*

1. **Preheat oven** to 350°F (175°C).
2. **Mix ingredients:** Beat butter and sugar, then mix in flour and salt.
3. **Roll dough into balls, press thumb in center, and fill with jam.**
4. **Bake** for 12-15 minutes.

## White Chocolate Macadamia Nut Cookies

*Ingredients:*

- 1 cup (226g) unsalted butter, softened
- 1 cup (200g) brown sugar
- ½ cup (100g) granulated sugar
- 2 eggs
- 1 teaspoon vanilla extract
- 2 ½ cups (315g) all-purpose flour
- 1 teaspoon baking soda
- ½ teaspoon salt
- 1 cup (170g) white chocolate chips
- ½ cup (75g) macadamia nuts, chopped

*Instructions:*

1. **Preheat oven** to 350°F (175°C).
2. **Mix ingredients:** Beat butter, sugars, eggs, and vanilla. Mix in dry ingredients.
3. **Fold in white chocolate and nuts.**
4. **Bake** for 10-12 minutes.

**Molasses Cookies**

*Ingredients:*

- ¾ cup (170g) unsalted butter, softened
- 1 cup (200g) brown sugar
- 1 egg
- ¼ cup (60ml) molasses
- 2 ½ cups (315g) all-purpose flour
- 2 teaspoons baking soda
- 1 teaspoon cinnamon
- 1 teaspoon ginger
- ½ teaspoon cloves
- ½ teaspoon salt

*Instructions:*

1. **Preheat oven** to 375°F (190°C).
2. **Mix wet ingredients:** Beat butter, sugar, egg, and molasses.
3. **Combine dry ingredients:** Mix flour, baking soda, and spices, then add to wet ingredients.
4. **Form dough into balls and roll in sugar.**
5. **Bake** for 10-12 minutes.

## Lemon Butter Cookies

*Ingredients:*

- 1 cup (226g) unsalted butter, softened
- ¾ cup (150g) granulated sugar
- 1 egg
- 1 teaspoon lemon zest
- 1 teaspoon lemon juice
- 2 ¼ cups (280g) all-purpose flour
- ½ teaspoon baking powder
- ½ teaspoon salt

*Instructions:*

1. **Preheat oven** to 350°F (175°C).
2. **Mix wet ingredients:** Beat butter, sugar, egg, lemon zest, and juice.
3. **Combine dry ingredients:** Mix flour, baking powder, and salt, then add to wet ingredients.
4. **Form dough into balls, flatten slightly.**
5. **Bake** for 10-12 minutes.

**Coconut Macaroons**

*Ingredients:*

- 3 cups (240g) shredded coconut
- ¾ cup (150g) granulated sugar
- 3 egg whites
- 1 teaspoon vanilla extract
- ¼ teaspoon salt

*Instructions:*

1. **Preheat oven** to 325°F (165°C).
2. **Mix ingredients:** Whisk egg whites, sugar, vanilla, and salt until frothy. Fold in coconut.
3. **Scoop onto baking sheet.**
4. **Bake** for 15-18 minutes until golden.

## Linzer Cookies

*Ingredients:*

- 1 cup (226g) unsalted butter, softened
- ¾ cup (150g) granulated sugar
- 1 egg
- 2 cups (250g) all-purpose flour
- 1 teaspoon cinnamon
- ½ cup (60g) almond flour
- ½ cup (120g) raspberry jam

*Instructions:*

1. **Preheat oven** to 350°F (175°C).
2. **Mix wet ingredients:** Beat butter, sugar, and egg.
3. **Combine dry ingredients:** Mix flour, cinnamon, and almond flour, then add to wet ingredients.
4. **Roll out dough, cut out shapes, and cut a small hole in half of them.**
5. **Bake** for 10-12 minutes, then sandwich with jam.

## Chocolate Crinkle Cookies

*Ingredients:*

- 1 cup (200g) granulated sugar
- ½ cup (120ml) vegetable oil
- 2 eggs
- 1 teaspoon vanilla extract
- 1 cup (120g) cocoa powder
- 1 ½ cups (190g) all-purpose flour
- 1 teaspoon baking powder
- ½ teaspoon salt
- ½ cup (60g) powdered sugar

*Instructions:*

1. **Preheat oven** to 350°F (175°C).
2. **Mix wet ingredients:** Beat sugar, oil, eggs, and vanilla.
3. **Combine dry ingredients:** Mix cocoa, flour, baking powder, and salt, then add to wet ingredients.
4. **Chill dough for 1 hour.**
5. **Roll in powdered sugar and bake** for 10-12 minutes.

**Meringue Cookies**

*Ingredients:*

- 3 egg whites
- ¾ cup (150g) granulated sugar
- ½ teaspoon vanilla extract
- ¼ teaspoon cream of tartar

*Instructions:*

1. **Preheat oven** to 225°F (110°C).
2. **Whip egg whites** with cream of tartar until soft peaks form.
3. **Slowly add sugar** while beating until stiff peaks form.
4. **Pipe onto a baking sheet.**
5. **Bake** for 1 ½ hours, then cool completely.

**Italian Wedding Cookies**

*Ingredients:*

- 1 cup (226g) unsalted butter, softened
- ½ cup (60g) powdered sugar
- 2 cups (250g) all-purpose flour
- 1 cup (120g) finely chopped pecans
- 1 teaspoon vanilla extract
- Extra powdered sugar for coating

*Instructions:*

1. **Preheat oven** to 350°F (175°C).
2. **Mix ingredients:** Beat butter, sugar, flour, pecans, and vanilla.
3. **Form small balls and bake** for 12-15 minutes.
4. **Roll in powdered sugar while warm.**

**Peanut Butter Blossoms**

*Ingredients:*

- 1 cup (256g) peanut butter
- ½ cup (113g) unsalted butter, softened
- ¾ cup (150g) brown sugar
- ½ cup (100g) granulated sugar
- 1 egg
- 1 teaspoon vanilla extract
- 1 ½ cups (190g) all-purpose flour
- 1 teaspoon baking soda
- ½ teaspoon salt
- 24 chocolate kisses

*Instructions:*

1. **Preheat oven** to 350°F (175°C).
2. **Mix ingredients:** Beat butter, peanut butter, sugars, egg, and vanilla.
3. **Combine dry ingredients:** Mix flour, baking soda, and salt, then add to wet ingredients.
4. **Form dough into balls and bake** for 10 minutes.
5. **Press a chocolate kiss into each cookie.**

**Pecan Sandies**

*Ingredients:*

- 1 cup (226g) unsalted butter, softened
- ½ cup (100g) granulated sugar
- 2 cups (250g) all-purpose flour
- 1 cup (120g) chopped pecans
- ½ teaspoon salt

*Instructions:*

1. **Preheat oven** to 350°F (175°C).
2. **Mix ingredients:** Beat butter and sugar, then mix in flour, pecans, and salt.
3. **Form dough into balls and flatten slightly.**
4. **Bake** for 12-15 minutes.

## Black and White Cookies

*Ingredients:*

- 1 cup (226g) unsalted butter, softened
- 1 cup (200g) granulated sugar
- 2 eggs
- ½ cup (120ml) milk
- 2 cups (250g) all-purpose flour
- 1 teaspoon baking powder
- ½ teaspoon salt

*For the Icing:*

- 1 cup (120g) powdered sugar
- 2 tablespoons milk
- ¼ cup (30g) cocoa powder

*Instructions:*

1. **Preheat oven** to 350°F (175°C).
2. **Mix ingredients:** Beat butter, sugar, eggs, and milk. Mix in dry ingredients.
3. **Scoop onto a baking sheet and bake** for 12-15 minutes.
4. **Make icing:** Mix powdered sugar with milk, divide in half, and add cocoa powder to one half.
5. **Frost half of each cookie with white and half with chocolate icing.**

**Rugelach**

*Ingredients:*

- 1 cup (226g) cream cheese, softened
- 1 cup (226g) unsalted butter, softened
- 2 cups (250g) all-purpose flour
- ½ cup (100g) sugar
- ½ cup (120g) jam
- ½ cup (50g) chopped walnuts

*Instructions:*

1. **Preheat oven** to 350°F (175°C).
2. **Make dough:** Mix cream cheese, butter, and flour. Chill for 1 hour.
3. **Roll out dough, spread with jam, and sprinkle sugar and walnuts.**
4. **Cut into triangles and roll into crescents.**
5. **Bake** for 15-18 minutes.

## Spritz Cookies

*Ingredients:*

- 1 cup (226g) unsalted butter, softened
- ¾ cup (150g) sugar
- 1 egg
- 2 ¼ cups (280g) all-purpose flour
- 1 teaspoon vanilla extract

*Instructions:*

1. **Preheat oven** to 375°F (190°C).
2. **Mix ingredients:** Beat butter, sugar, egg, and vanilla.
3. **Add flour and mix until smooth.**
4. **Pipe dough onto baking sheet.**
5. **Bake** for 10-12 minutes.

**Anzac Biscuits**

*Ingredients:*

- 1 cup (90g) rolled oats
- 1 cup (120g) all-purpose flour
- ¾ cup (150g) brown sugar
- ½ cup (40g) shredded coconut
- ½ cup (113g) unsalted butter
- 2 tablespoons golden syrup (or honey)
- ½ teaspoon baking soda
- 2 tablespoons boiling water

*Instructions:*

1. **Preheat oven** to 350°F (175°C).
2. **Mix dry ingredients:** Combine oats, flour, sugar, and coconut.
3. **Melt butter & syrup:** Stir in baking soda dissolved in boiling water.
4. **Combine & shape dough:** Mix wet and dry ingredients, form small balls.
5. **Bake** for 12-15 minutes.

**Butter Pecan Cookies**

*Ingredients:*

- 1 cup (226g) unsalted butter, softened
- ½ cup (100g) brown sugar
- ½ cup (100g) granulated sugar
- 1 egg
- 2 teaspoons vanilla extract
- 2 cups (250g) all-purpose flour
- ½ teaspoon baking soda
- ½ teaspoon salt
- 1 cup (120g) chopped pecans

*Instructions:*

1. **Preheat oven** to 350°F (175°C).
2. **Mix wet ingredients:** Beat butter, sugars, egg, and vanilla.
3. **Combine dry ingredients:** Mix flour, baking soda, and salt, then add to wet ingredients.
4. **Fold in pecans & scoop dough onto a baking sheet.**
5. **Bake** for 10-12 minutes.

## No-Bake Chocolate Oatmeal Cookies

*Ingredients:*

- ½ cup (113g) unsalted butter
- 2 cups (400g) granulated sugar
- ½ cup (120ml) milk
- ¼ cup (25g) cocoa powder
- ½ cup (130g) peanut butter
- 3 cups (270g) rolled oats
- 1 teaspoon vanilla extract

*Instructions:*

1. **Melt butter, sugar, milk, and cocoa powder** in a saucepan, bring to a boil.
2. **Remove from heat, stir in peanut butter, oats, and vanilla.**
3. **Scoop onto parchment paper & let set** for 30 minutes.

**Raspberry Almond Thumbprints**

*Ingredients:*

- 1 cup (226g) unsalted butter, softened
- ½ cup (100g) granulated sugar
- 1 egg yolk
- 1 teaspoon almond extract
- 2 cups (250g) all-purpose flour
- ½ cup (120g) raspberry jam
- ½ cup (50g) chopped almonds

*Instructions:*

1. **Preheat oven** to 350°F (175°C).
2. **Mix wet ingredients:** Beat butter, sugar, egg yolk, and almond extract.
3. **Mix in flour, form dough balls, and press thumb into center.**
4. **Fill with raspberry jam & sprinkle almonds.**
5. **Bake** for 12-15 minutes.

**Pumpkin Spice Cookies**

*Ingredients:*

- ½ cup (113g) unsalted butter, softened
- 1 cup (200g) brown sugar
- ½ cup (120g) pumpkin purée
- 1 egg
- 1 teaspoon vanilla extract
- 2 cups (250g) all-purpose flour
- 1 teaspoon baking soda
- 1 teaspoon cinnamon
- ½ teaspoon nutmeg
- ½ teaspoon salt

*Instructions:*

1. **Preheat oven** to 350°F (175°C).
2. **Mix wet ingredients:** Beat butter, sugar, pumpkin, egg, and vanilla.
3. **Combine dry ingredients:** Mix flour, baking soda, spices, and salt, then add to wet ingredients.
4. **Scoop dough onto baking sheet.**
5. **Bake** for 12-14 minutes.

**Cinnamon Sugar Palmiers**

*Ingredients:*

- 1 sheet puff pastry, thawed
- ¼ cup (50g) granulated sugar
- 1 teaspoon cinnamon

*Instructions:*

1. **Preheat oven** to 400°F (200°C).
2. **Roll out pastry & sprinkle with cinnamon sugar.**
3. **Fold both edges towards center twice to create a log shape.**
4. **Chill for 15 minutes, slice, and bake** for 12-15 minutes.

**Florentine Lace Cookies**

*Ingredients:*

- ½ cup (113g) unsalted butter
- ⅔ cup (150g) brown sugar
- 2 tablespoons honey
- 1 cup (90g) finely chopped almonds
- 2 tablespoons all-purpose flour
- ¼ teaspoon salt

*Instructions:*

1. **Preheat oven** to 350°F (175°C).
2. **Melt butter, sugar, and honey** in a saucepan, then stir in almonds, flour, and salt.
3. **Drop small spoonfuls onto baking sheet.**
4. **Bake** for 8-10 minutes.

**Honey Lavender Shortbread**

*Ingredients:*

- 1 cup (226g) unsalted butter, softened
- ½ cup (100g) granulated sugar
- 2 cups (250g) all-purpose flour
- 1 tablespoon honey
- 1 teaspoon dried lavender

*Instructions:*

1. **Preheat oven** to 325°F (165°C).
2. **Mix butter, sugar, and honey.**
3. **Add flour and lavender, form dough, chill for 30 minutes.**
4. **Roll out and cut shapes.**
5. **Bake** for 15-18 minutes.

## Viennese Whirls

*Ingredients:*

- 1 cup (226g) unsalted butter, softened
- ½ cup (100g) powdered sugar
- 1 ¼ cups (160g) all-purpose flour
- ¼ cup (30g) cornstarch
- 1 teaspoon vanilla extract

*For the Filling:*

- ½ cup (115g) butter, softened
- 1 cup (120g) powdered sugar
- 2 tablespoons raspberry jam

*Instructions:*

1. **Preheat oven** to 375°F (190°C).
2. **Mix ingredients** and pipe onto baking sheet.
3. **Bake** for 10-12 minutes.
4. **Fill with buttercream and jam.**

## Chocolate-Dipped Coconut Cookies

*Ingredients:*

- 2 cups (160g) shredded coconut
- ½ cup (100g) granulated sugar
- 2 egg whites
- ½ teaspoon vanilla extract
- ½ cup (90g) dark chocolate, melted

*Instructions:*

1. **Preheat oven** to 325°F (165°C).
2. **Mix coconut, sugar, egg whites, and vanilla.**
3. **Scoop onto baking sheet.**
4. **Bake** for 15-18 minutes.
5. **Dip bottoms in melted chocolate.**

**Tahini Sesame Cookies**

*Ingredients:*

- ½ cup (120g) tahini
- ½ cup (113g) unsalted butter, softened
- ½ cup (100g) brown sugar
- ½ cup (100g) granulated sugar
- 1 egg
- 1 teaspoon vanilla extract
- 1 ½ cups (190g) all-purpose flour
- ½ teaspoon baking soda
- ½ teaspoon salt
- ¼ cup (30g) sesame seeds

*Instructions:*

1. **Preheat oven** to 350°F (175°C).
2. **Mix wet ingredients:** Beat tahini, butter, sugars, egg, and vanilla.
3. **Combine dry ingredients:** Mix flour, baking soda, and salt, then add to wet ingredients.
4. **Form dough into balls, roll in sesame seeds.**
5. **Bake** for 12-14 minutes.

## Apple Cider Cookies

*Ingredients:*

- ½ cup (113g) unsalted butter, softened
- ¾ cup (150g) brown sugar
- 1 egg
- ¼ cup (60ml) apple cider
- 2 cups (250g) all-purpose flour
- ½ teaspoon baking soda
- ½ teaspoon cinnamon
- ¼ teaspoon nutmeg
- ½ teaspoon salt

*Instructions:*

1. **Preheat oven** to 350°F (175°C).
2. **Mix wet ingredients:** Beat butter, sugar, egg, and apple cider.
3. **Combine dry ingredients:** Mix flour, baking soda, spices, and salt, then add to wet ingredients.
4. **Scoop dough onto a baking sheet.**
5. **Bake** for 10-12 minutes.

**Bourbon Pecan Cookies**

*Ingredients:*

- ½ cup (113g) unsalted butter, softened
- ½ cup (100g) brown sugar
- ¼ cup (50g) granulated sugar
- 1 egg
- 2 tablespoons bourbon
- 1 ½ cups (190g) all-purpose flour
- ½ teaspoon baking soda
- ½ teaspoon cinnamon
- 1 cup (120g) chopped pecans

*Instructions:*

1. **Preheat oven** to 350°F (175°C).
2. **Mix wet ingredients:** Beat butter, sugars, egg, and bourbon.
3. **Combine dry ingredients:** Mix flour, baking soda, and cinnamon, then add to wet ingredients.
4. **Fold in pecans and scoop dough onto a baking sheet.**
5. **Bake** for 10-12 minutes.

**Cornmeal Lime Cookies**

*Ingredients:*

- ½ cup (113g) unsalted butter, softened
- ¾ cup (150g) granulated sugar
- 1 egg
- 1 teaspoon lime zest
- 1 ½ cups (190g) all-purpose flour
- ½ cup (75g) cornmeal
- ½ teaspoon baking powder
- ¼ teaspoon salt

*Instructions:*

1. **Preheat oven** to 350°F (175°C).
2. **Mix wet ingredients:** Beat butter, sugar, egg, and lime zest.
3. **Combine dry ingredients:** Mix flour, cornmeal, baking powder, and salt, then add to wet ingredients.
4. **Form dough into balls and place on a baking sheet.**
5. **Bake** for 12-14 minutes.

**Chocolate-Dipped Orange Biscotti**

*Ingredients:*

- ½ cup (113g) unsalted butter, softened
- ¾ cup (150g) granulated sugar
- 2 eggs
- 1 teaspoon orange zest
- 2 cups (250g) all-purpose flour
- 1 teaspoon baking powder
- ½ cup (90g) dark chocolate, melted

*Instructions:*

1. **Preheat oven** to 350°F (175°C).
2. **Mix wet ingredients:** Beat butter, sugar, eggs, and orange zest.
3. **Combine dry ingredients:** Mix flour and baking powder, then add to wet ingredients.
4. **Shape into logs and bake** for 25 minutes.
5. **Slice logs, bake again for 10 minutes, then dip in chocolate.**

## Hazelnut Crescent Cookies

*Ingredients:*

- 1 cup (226g) unsalted butter, softened
- ½ cup (100g) granulated sugar
- 2 cups (250g) all-purpose flour
- 1 cup (120g) ground hazelnuts
- ½ teaspoon vanilla extract
- Powdered sugar for coating

*Instructions:*

1. **Preheat oven** to 350°F (175°C).
2. **Mix ingredients:** Beat butter, sugar, flour, hazelnuts, and vanilla.
3. **Shape dough into crescents and bake** for 12-15 minutes.
4. **Roll warm cookies in powdered sugar.**

**Banana Oatmeal Cookies**

*Ingredients:*

- ½ cup (113g) unsalted butter, softened
- ¾ cup (150g) brown sugar
- 1 ripe banana, mashed
- 1 egg
- 1 teaspoon vanilla extract
- 1 ½ cups (135g) rolled oats
- 1 cup (125g) all-purpose flour
- ½ teaspoon baking soda
- ½ teaspoon cinnamon

*Instructions:*

1. **Preheat oven** to 350°F (175°C).
2. **Mix wet ingredients:** Beat butter, sugar, banana, egg, and vanilla.
3. **Combine dry ingredients:** Mix oats, flour, baking soda, and cinnamon, then add to wet ingredients.
4. **Scoop onto baking sheet and bake** for 10-12 minutes.

## Maple Walnut Cookies

*Ingredients:*

- ½ cup (113g) unsalted butter, softened
- ½ cup (100g) brown sugar
- ¼ cup (60ml) maple syrup
- 1 egg
- 1 teaspoon vanilla extract
- 2 cups (250g) all-purpose flour
- ½ teaspoon baking soda
- ½ teaspoon salt
- ¾ cup (90g) chopped walnuts

*Instructions:*

1. **Preheat oven** to 350°F (175°C).
2. **Mix wet ingredients:** Beat butter, sugar, maple syrup, egg, and vanilla.
3. **Combine dry ingredients:** Mix flour, baking soda, and salt, then add to wet ingredients.
4. **Fold in walnuts and scoop onto baking sheet.**
5. **Bake** for 10-12 minutes.

**Matcha Green Tea Cookies**

*Ingredients:*

- 1 cup (226g) unsalted butter, softened
- ¾ cup (150g) granulated sugar
- 2 cups (250g) all-purpose flour
- 1 tablespoon matcha powder
- ½ teaspoon salt

*Instructions:*

1. **Preheat oven** to 325°F (165°C).
2. **Mix butter and sugar.**
3. **Add flour, matcha, and salt, mix until dough forms.**
4. **Roll out dough, cut into shapes.**
5. **Bake** for 12-14 minutes.

## Brown Butter Chocolate Chip Cookies

*Ingredients:*

- ¾ cup (170g) unsalted butter
- ¾ cup (150g) brown sugar
- ¼ cup (50g) granulated sugar
- 1 egg + 1 egg yolk
- 1 teaspoon vanilla extract
- 2 cups (250g) all-purpose flour
- ½ teaspoon baking soda
- ½ teaspoon salt
- 1 cup (170g) chocolate chips

*Instructions:*

1. **Brown butter in a pan, let cool.**
2. **Mix wet ingredients:** Beat browned butter, sugars, eggs, and vanilla.
3. **Combine dry ingredients:** Mix flour, baking soda, and salt, then add to wet ingredients.
4. **Fold in chocolate chips and scoop onto a baking sheet.**
5. **Bake** at 350°F (175°C) for 10-12 minutes.

**White Chocolate Cranberry Cookies**

*Ingredients:*

- ½ cup (113g) unsalted butter, softened
- ½ cup (100g) brown sugar
- ¼ cup (50g) granulated sugar
- 1 egg
- 1 teaspoon vanilla extract
- 1 ½ cups (190g) all-purpose flour
- ½ teaspoon baking soda
- ½ teaspoon salt
- ¾ cup (130g) white chocolate chips
- ½ cup (75g) dried cranberries

*Instructions:*

1. **Preheat oven** to 350°F (175°C).
2. **Mix wet ingredients:** Beat butter, sugars, egg, and vanilla.
3. **Combine dry ingredients:** Mix flour, baking soda, and salt, then add to wet ingredients.
4. **Fold in white chocolate and cranberries.**
5. **Bake** for 10-12 minutes.

**Classic Whoopie Pies**

*Ingredients:*

- **For the Cookies:**
    - 2 cups (250g) all-purpose flour
    - ½ cup (50g) cocoa powder
    - 1 teaspoon baking soda
    - ½ teaspoon salt
    - ½ cup (113g) unsalted butter, softened
    - 1 cup (200g) brown sugar
    - 1 egg
    - 1 teaspoon vanilla extract
    - 1 cup (240ml) buttermilk
- **For the Filling:**
    - ½ cup (113g) unsalted butter, softened
    - 1 ½ cups (180g) powdered sugar
    - 1 cup (100g) marshmallow fluff
    - 1 teaspoon vanilla extract

*Instructions:*

1. **Preheat oven** to 350°F (175°C).
2. **Make the batter:** Beat butter and sugar, add egg and vanilla, then mix in flour, cocoa, baking soda, salt, and buttermilk.
3. **Scoop batter onto a baking sheet and bake** for 10-12 minutes.
4. **Make the filling:** Beat butter, powdered sugar, marshmallow fluff, and vanilla until fluffy.
5. **Assemble the whoopie pies** by sandwiching filling between two cookies.

**Peanut Butter Oatmeal Cookies**

*Ingredients:*

- ½ cup (113g) unsalted butter, softened
- ½ cup (100g) brown sugar
- ½ cup (100g) granulated sugar
- ½ cup (128g) peanut butter
- 1 egg
- 1 teaspoon vanilla extract
- 1 cup (125g) all-purpose flour
- ½ teaspoon baking soda
- ½ teaspoon salt
- 1 cup (90g) rolled oats

*Instructions:*

1. **Preheat oven** to 350°F (175°C).
2. **Mix wet ingredients:** Beat butter, sugars, peanut butter, egg, and vanilla.
3. **Combine dry ingredients:** Mix flour, baking soda, and salt, then add to wet ingredients.
4. **Fold in oats and scoop dough onto a baking sheet.**
5. **Bake** for 10-12 minutes.

## Espresso Chocolate Cookies

*Ingredients:*

- ½ cup (113g) unsalted butter, softened
- ½ cup (100g) brown sugar
- ¼ cup (50g) granulated sugar
- 1 egg
- 1 teaspoon vanilla extract
- 1 cup (125g) all-purpose flour
- ½ teaspoon baking soda
- 1 tablespoon espresso powder
- ½ teaspoon salt
- 1 cup (170g) chocolate chips

*Instructions:*

1. **Preheat oven** to 350°F (175°C).
2. **Mix wet ingredients:** Beat butter, sugars, egg, and vanilla.
3. **Combine dry ingredients:** Mix flour, baking soda, espresso powder, and salt, then add to wet ingredients.
4. **Fold in chocolate chips and scoop dough onto a baking sheet.**
5. **Bake** for 10-12 minutes.

**Red Velvet Crinkle Cookies**

*Ingredients:*

- ½ cup (113g) unsalted butter, softened
- ¾ cup (150g) granulated sugar
- 1 egg
- 1 teaspoon vanilla extract
- 1 ½ cups (190g) all-purpose flour
- ¼ cup (25g) cocoa powder
- 1 teaspoon baking powder
- ½ teaspoon salt
- 1 tablespoon red food coloring
- ½ cup (60g) powdered sugar (for rolling)

*Instructions:*

1. **Preheat oven** to 350°F (175°C).
2. **Mix wet ingredients:** Beat butter, sugar, egg, vanilla, and food coloring.
3. **Combine dry ingredients:** Mix flour, cocoa, baking powder, and salt, then add to wet ingredients.
4. **Chill dough for 30 minutes.**
5. **Roll in powdered sugar and bake** for 10-12 minutes.

## Caramel-Stuffed Chocolate Cookies

*Ingredients:*

- ½ cup (113g) unsalted butter, softened
- ½ cup (100g) brown sugar
- ¼ cup (50g) granulated sugar
- 1 egg
- 1 teaspoon vanilla extract
- 1 cup (125g) all-purpose flour
- ¼ cup (30g) cocoa powder
- ½ teaspoon baking soda
- ½ teaspoon salt
- 12 soft caramels

*Instructions:*

1. **Preheat oven** to 350°F (175°C).
2. **Mix wet ingredients:** Beat butter, sugars, egg, and vanilla.
3. **Combine dry ingredients:** Mix flour, cocoa, baking soda, and salt, then add to wet ingredients.
4. **Form dough balls, place a caramel in the center, and seal.**
5. **Bake** for 10-12 minutes.

## S'mores Cookies

*Ingredients:*

- ½ cup (113g) unsalted butter, softened
- ½ cup (100g) brown sugar
- ¼ cup (50g) granulated sugar
- 1 egg
- 1 teaspoon vanilla extract
- 1 cup (125g) all-purpose flour
- ½ teaspoon baking soda
- ½ teaspoon salt
- ½ cup (85g) chocolate chips
- ½ cup (30g) mini marshmallows
- ½ cup (60g) crushed graham crackers

*Instructions:*

1. **Preheat oven** to 350°F (175°C).
2. **Mix wet ingredients:** Beat butter, sugars, egg, and vanilla.
3. **Combine dry ingredients:** Mix flour, baking soda, and salt, then add to wet ingredients.
4. **Fold in chocolate chips, marshmallows, and graham crackers.**
5. **Bake** for 10-12 minutes.

www.ingramcontent.com/pod-product-compliance
Lightning Source LLC
LaVergne TN
LVHW081333060526
838201LV00055B/2623